Th[...]k

Music by
John Kander

Lyrics by
Fred Ebb

Music Transcribed by: Paul McKibbins

The Rink A new musical

Jules Fisher, Roger Berlind and Joan Cullman, Milbro Prods., Kenneth-John Prods. with Jonathan Farkas present Chita Rivera, Liza Minnelli in The Rink. Book by Terrence McNally. Music by John Kander. Lyrics by Fred Ebb. With Jason Alexander, Ronn Carroll, Scott Ellis, Kim Hauser, Scott Holmes, Mel Johnson, Jr., Frank Mastrocola. Scenery designed by Peter Larkin. Costumes designed by Theoni V. Aldredge. Lighting designed by Marc B. Weiss. Sound designed by Otts Munderloh. Hair and make-up by J. Roy Helland. Musical director: Paul Gemignani. Dance arrangements by Tom Fay. Orchestrations by Michael Gibson. Assistant choreographer: Tina Paul. Associate producers: Tina Chen, Jujamcyn Theatres. General management: Marvin A. Krauss. Casting: Johnson-Liff Associates. Press representation: Merle Debuskey.
Executive producer: Robin Ullman. Music Publisher: Tommy Valando. Choreography by Graciela Daniele.
Directed by A. J. Antoon.

ISBN 0-634-08478-X

CA

CARLIN AMERICA

EXCLUSIVELY DISTRIBUTED BY

HAL•LEONARD®
CORPORATION

7777 W. BLUEMOUND RD. P.O. BOX 13819 MILWAUKEE, WI 53213

Visit Hal Leonard Online at
www.halleonard.com

JOHN KANDER

FRED EBB and **JOHN KANDER**
(Words and Music). For the theatre: *Flora, the Red Menace; Cabaret; The Happy Time; Zorba; 70 Girls 70; Chicago; The Act; Woman of the Year.* For films: *Cabaret; Norman Rockwell: A Short Subject; Lucky Lady; New York, New York; Funny Lady; A Matter of Time; French Post Cards.* For television: "Liza" (Liza Minnelli), "Ol' Blue Eyes Is Back" (Frank Sinatra), "Liza with a Z" (Liza Minnelli), "Gypsy in My Soul" (Shirley MacLaine), "Goldie and Liza Together" (Goldie Hawn and Liza Minnelli), "Baryshnikov on Broadway" (Mikhail Baryshnikov).

FRED EBB

The Rink

Contents

COLORED LIGHTS

Words by
FRED EBB

Music by
JOHN KANDER

I was

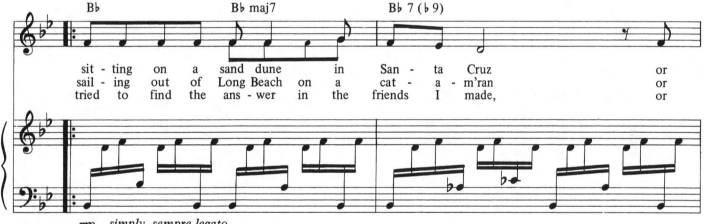

Bb   Bb maj7   Bb 7 (b9)

sit - ting   on   a   sand dune   in   San - ta Cruz   or
sail - ing   out   of   Long Beach   on   a   cat - a - m'ran   or
tried   to   find   the ans - wer   in   the   friends   I   made,   or

mp   simply, sempre legato

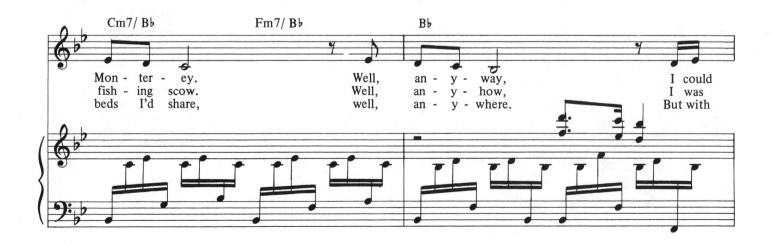

Cm7/ Bb   Fm7/ Bb   Bb

Mon — ter - ey.   Well,   an — y — way,   I could
fish — ing scow.   Well,   an — y — how,   I was
beds   I'd share,   well,   an — y - where.   But with

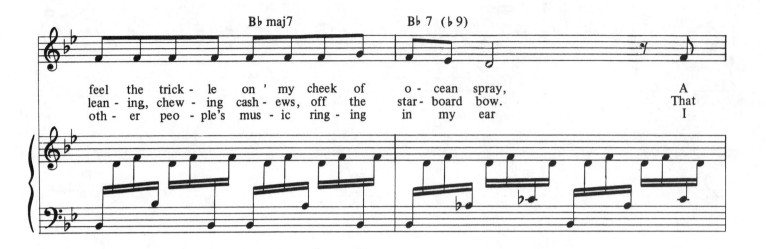

feel the trick - le on ' my cheek of o - cean spray,
lean - ing, chew - ing cash - ews, off the star - board bow.
oth - er peo - ple's mus - ic ring - ing in my ear

A
That
I

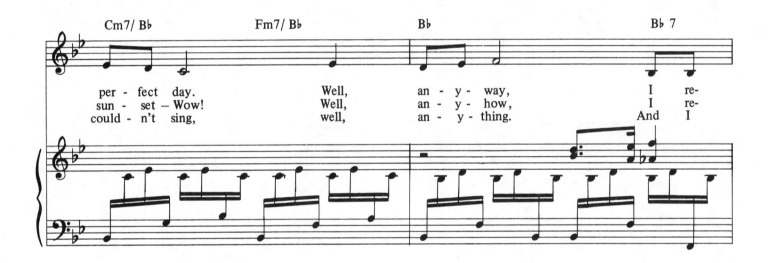

per - fect day. Well, an - y - way,
sun - set — Wow! Well, an - y - how,
could - n't sing, well, an - y - thing.

I
I re -
And I re -

mem - ber that I turned to Sam and said . . .
mem - ber tell - ing Jo - ey, "God, you're sweet!"
thought if I could just be twelve a - gain,

Or was it
Or was it
or was it

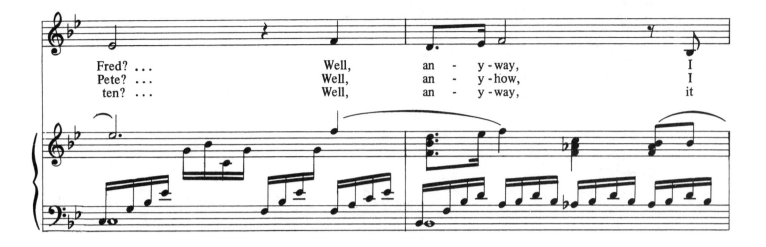

Fred? ... Well, an - y -way, I
Pete? ... Well, an - y -how, I
ten? ... Well, an - y -way, it

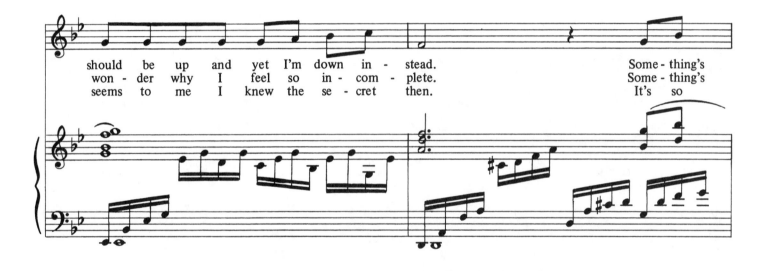

should be up and yet I'm down in - stead. Some - thing's
won - der why I feel so in - com - plete. Some - thing's
seems to me I knew the se - cret then. It's so

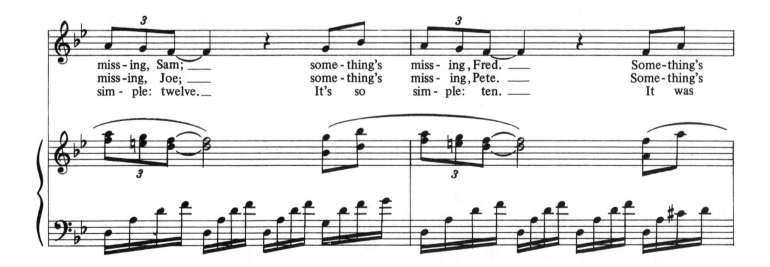

miss - ing, Sam; ___ some - thing's miss - ing, Fred. ___ Some - thing's
miss - ing, Joe; ___ some - thing's miss - ing, Pete. ___ Some - thing's
sim - ple: twelve. ___ It's so sim - ple: ten. ___ It was

miss - ing here.
miss - ing here.
sim - ple there.

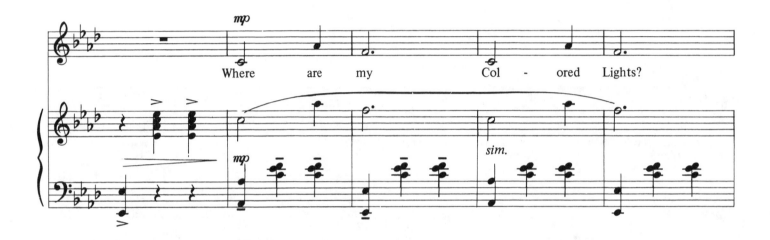

Where are my Col - ored Lights?

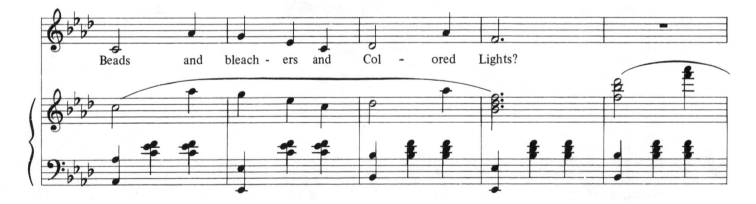

Beads and bleach - ers and Col - ored Lights?

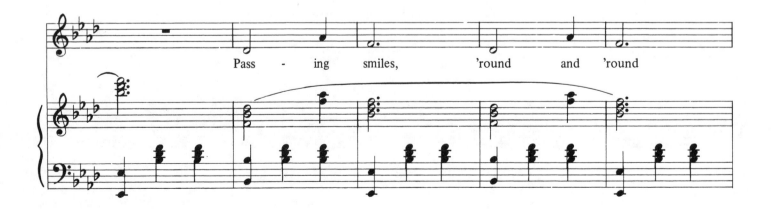

Pass - ing smiles, 'round and 'round

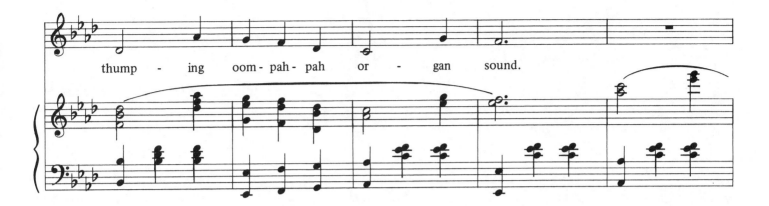

thump - ing oom - pah - pah or - gan sound.

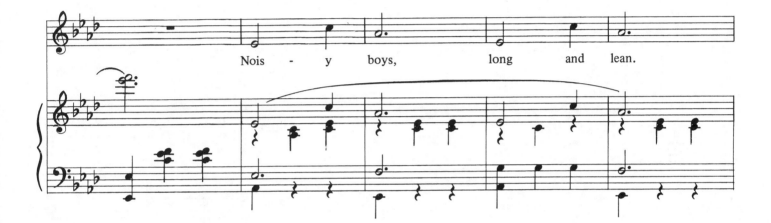

Nois - y boys, long and lean.

Gig - gles of girls in the mez - za - nine.

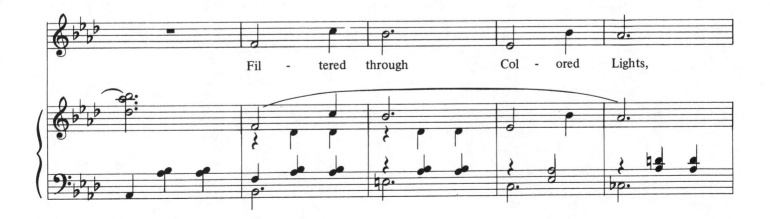

Fil - tered through Col - ored Lights,

10

Gold and am-ber and green.

I was
And I

Coda

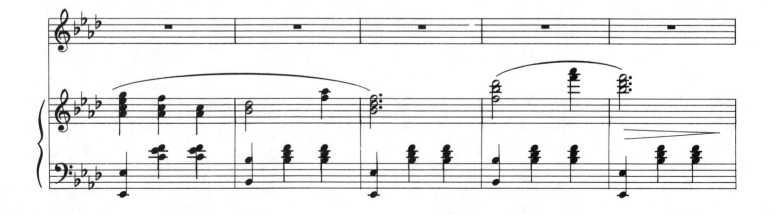

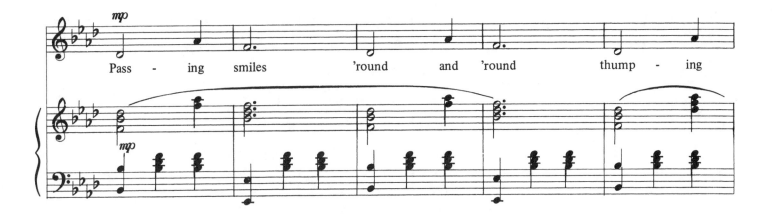

Pass - ing smiles 'round and 'round thump - ing

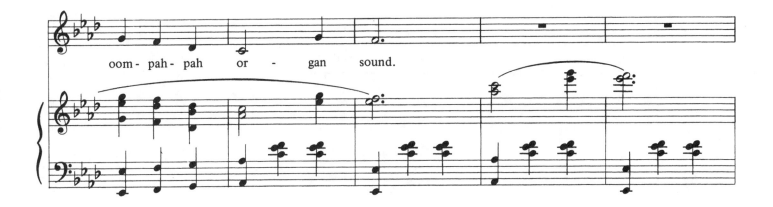

oom - pah - pah or - gan sound.

Nois - y boys, long and lean, Gig - gles of

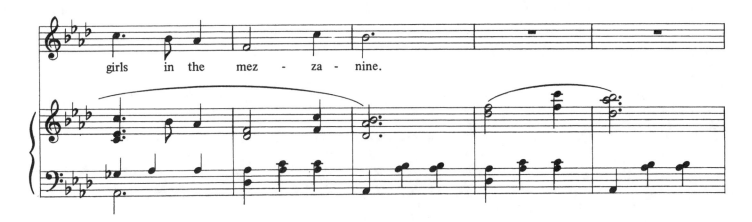

girls in the mez - za - nine.

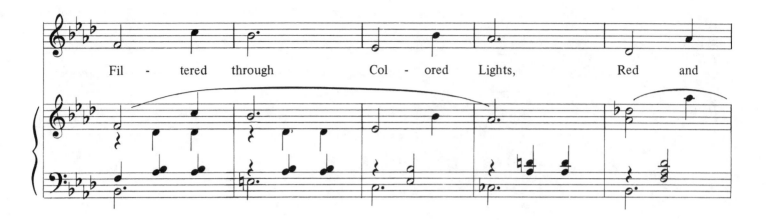

Fil - tered through Col - ored Lights, Red and

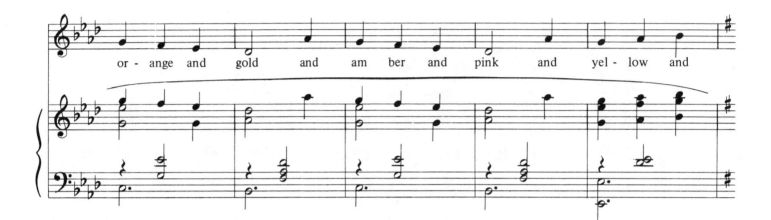

or - ange and gold and am ber and pink and yel - low and

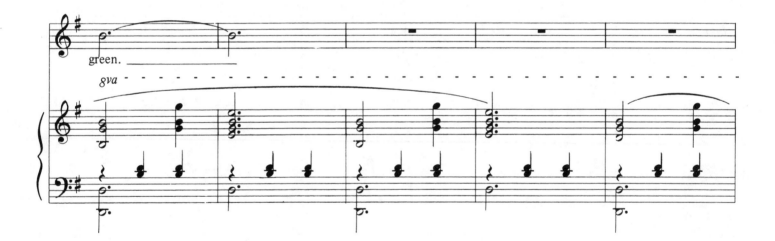

green.

8va

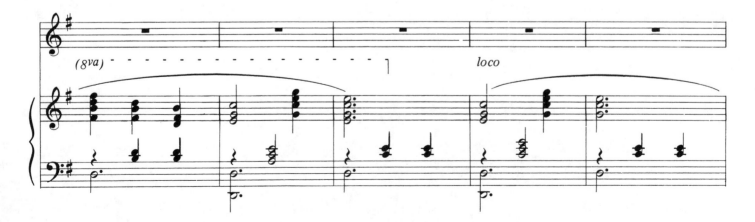

(8va)   *loco*

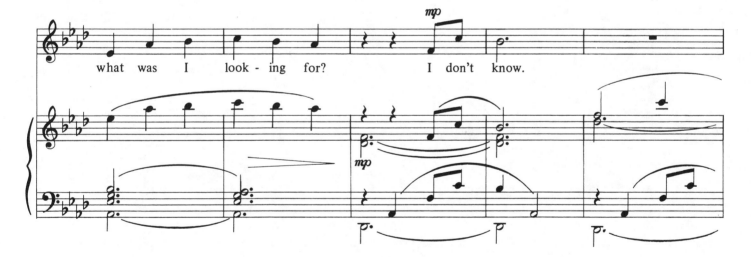

Leav - ing home years a - go

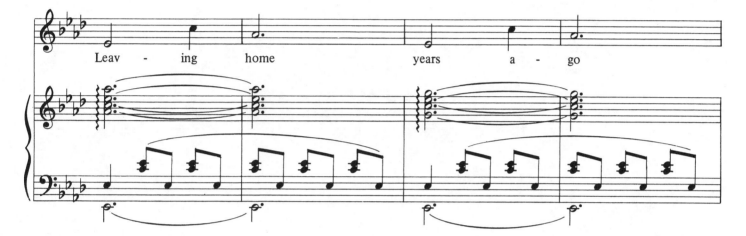

what was I look - ing for? I don't know.

I can't re - call well, an - y way.

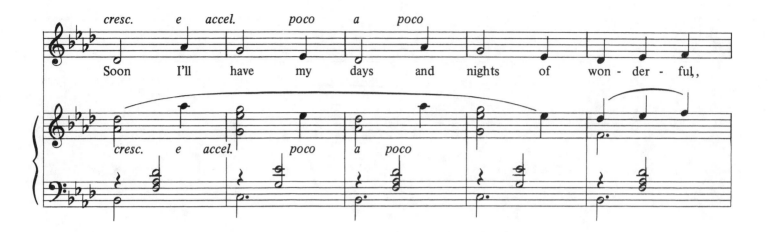

Soon I'll have my days and nights of won - der - ful,

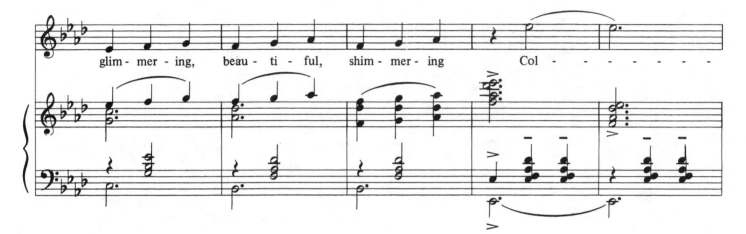

glim - mer - ing, beau - ti - ful, shim - mer - ing Col - - - - -

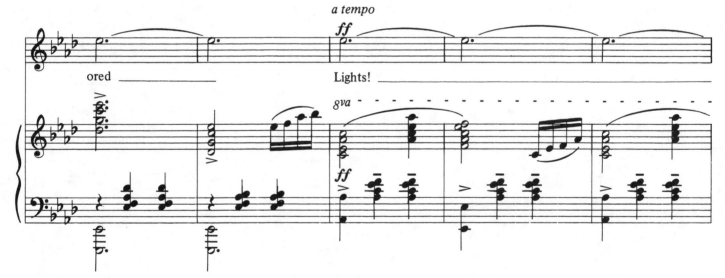

ored _____ Lights! _____

CHIEF COOK AND BOTTLE WASHER

Words by
FRED EBB

Music by
JOHN KANDER

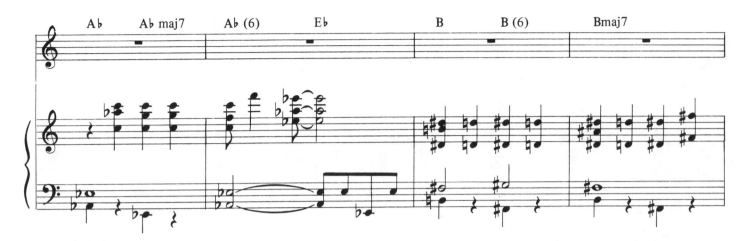

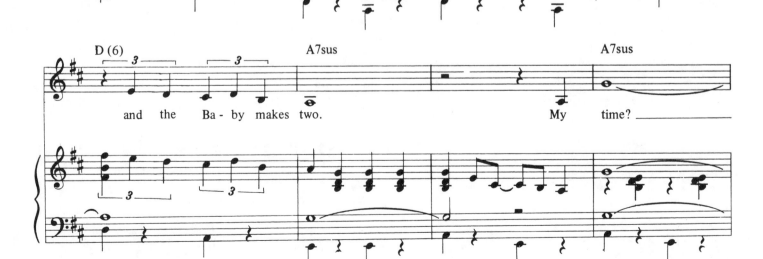

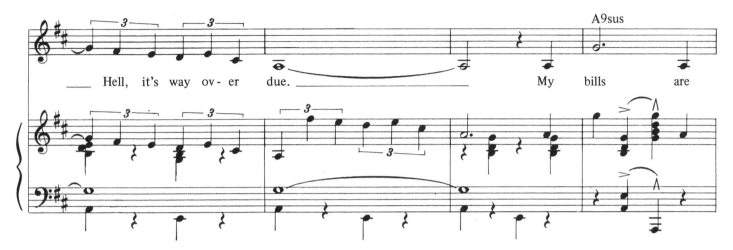

Hell, it's way ov - er due. _____ My bills are

Molto rallentando

paid. My fu - ture's made.

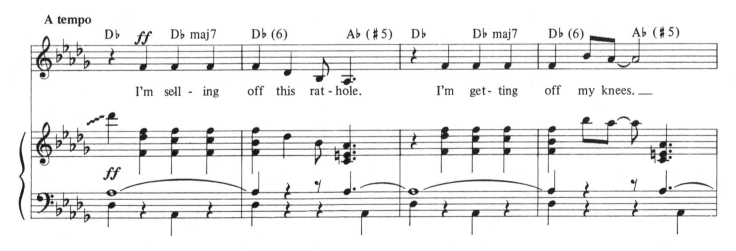

A tempo

I'm sell - ing off this rat - hole. I'm get - ting off my knees. __

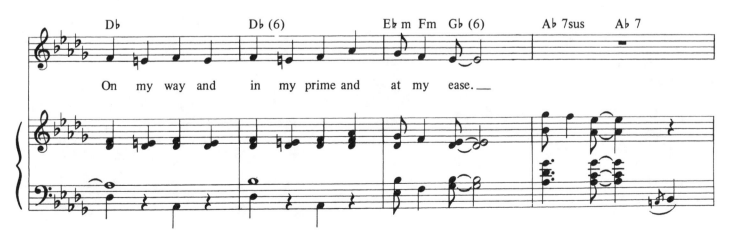

On my way and in my prime and at my ease. __

BLUE CRYSTAL

Words by
FRED EBB

Music by
JOHN KANDER

long, ex - haust - ing trip, but I fig - ured you were worth it.

Still . . . on - ly three days?! That's per - fect - ly a - maz - ing!

I've been to the

Moon and back and you know what they've got up there? Blue

Presto

E

Crys - tal.

Freely

E/ B

I met a man on the Moon who sits a - round

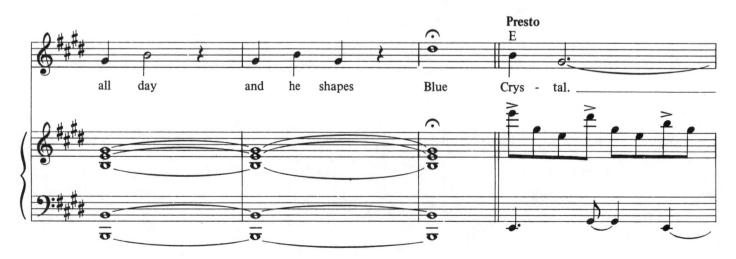

all day and he shapes Blue Crys - tal.

Presto

E

He's got a

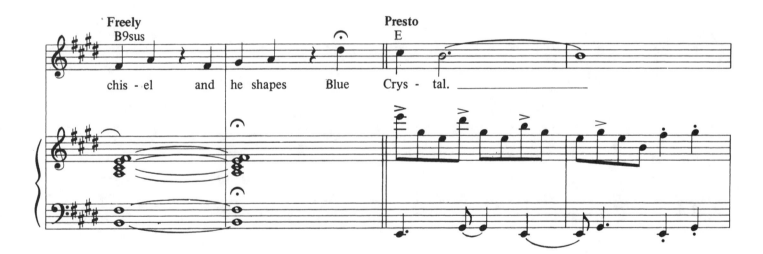

B9sus   B (6)   B9sus   B (6)   B9sus   B (6)

fur - nace   and a   blow - er   and a   mal - let   and a

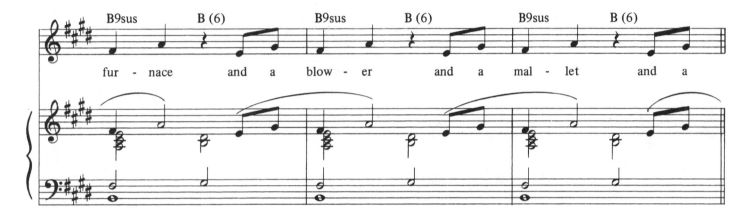

Freely
B9sus

Presto
E

chis - el   and   he shapes   Blue Crys - tal. _____

B9sus

So   I   said,   "I want a pres - ent

for a ver-y spe-cial la-dy, that you can't buy____

____ in a store." And he sold me eight gob-lets

and there aren't an-y-more in the whole wide

world. Yes

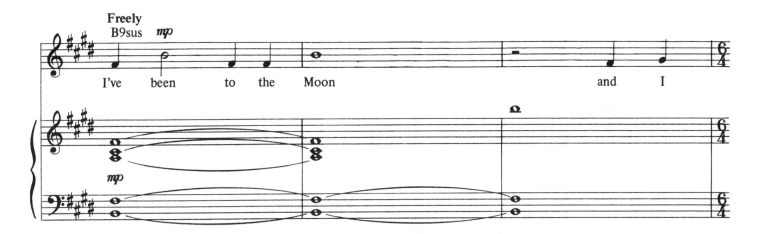

I've been to the Moon and I

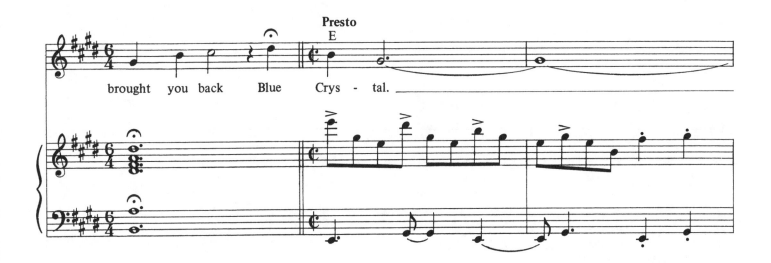

brought you back Blue Crys - tal.

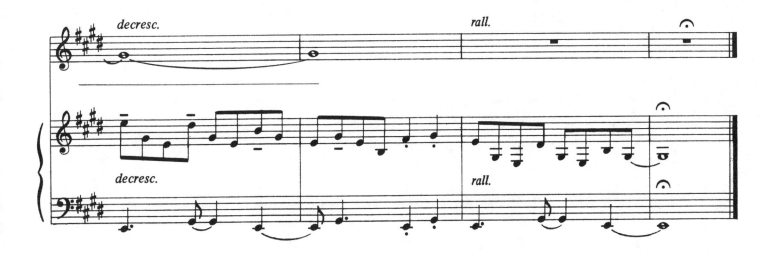

UNDER THE ROLLER COASTER

Words by
FRED EBB

Music by
JOHN KANDER

Under The Rol-ler-coast-er, next to the Jun-gle Ride, _____
(2nd time tacet)

right of the Cat-er-pil-lar, left of the Wat-er-slide, _____
(2nd time sung)

back of the Sil - ver Streak, in front of the Whip, Two blocks from Cas- ey's In - ter-

plan - e - ta - ry Trip.   Fa -
                                                                             Fa -

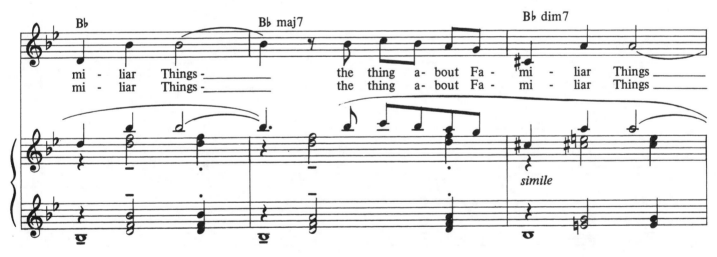

mi - liar Things _____   the thing a- bout Fa - mi - liar Things _____
mi - liar Things _____   the thing a- bout Fa - mi - liar Things _____

_____ is how you keep i - ma - gin - ing _____ they'll nev- er go a -
_____ is how you keep i - ma - gin - ing _____ they'll nev- er go a -

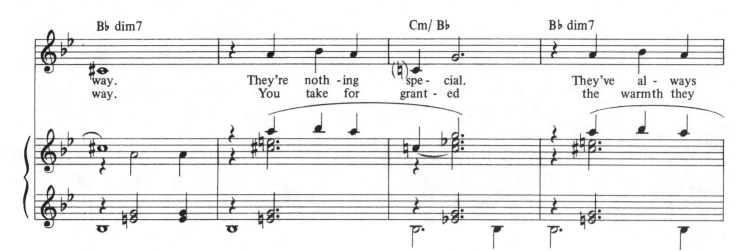

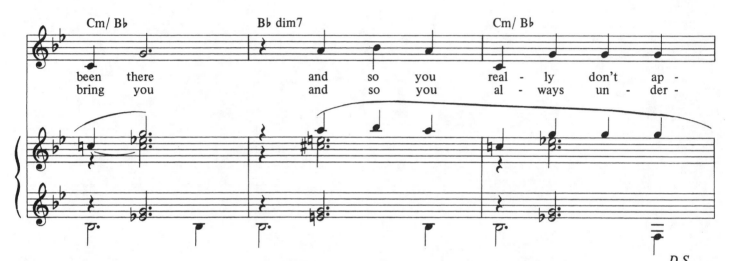

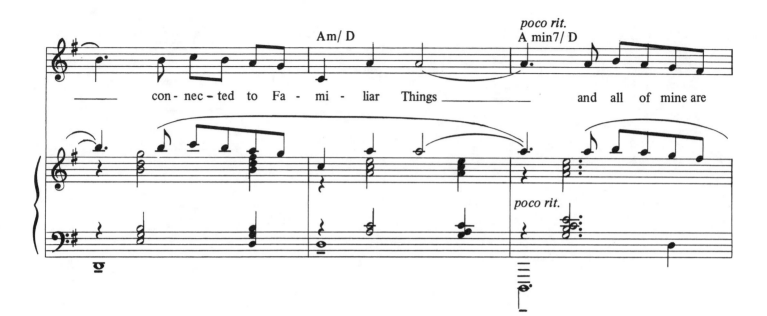

con - nec – ted to Fa - mi - liar Things _____ and all of mine are

Am/ D

poco rit.

A min7/ D

a tempo

G

here _____

p

Un - der The Rol - ler coast - er

p staccato

next to the Jun - gle Ride. _____

decresc.

pp

WE CAN MAKE IT

Words by
FRED EBB

Music by
JOHN KANDER

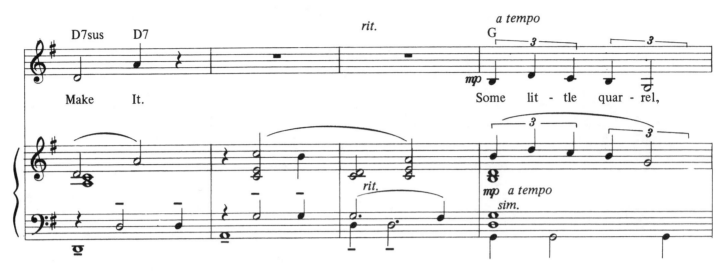

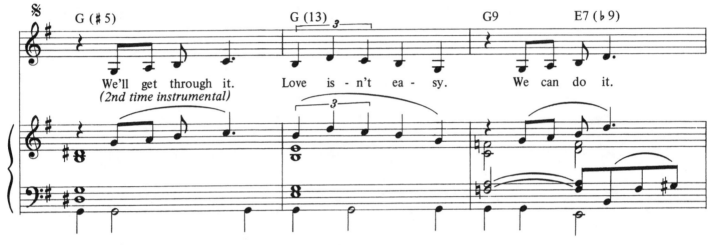

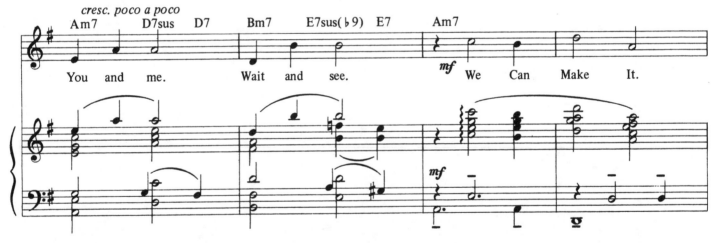

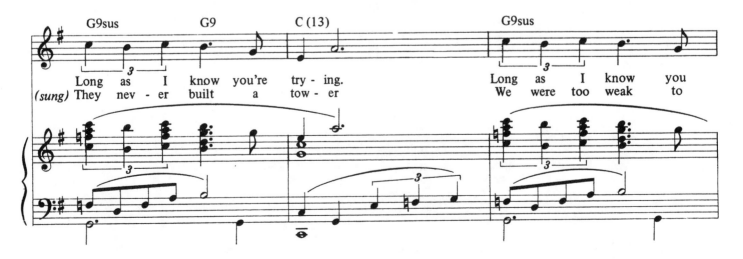

38

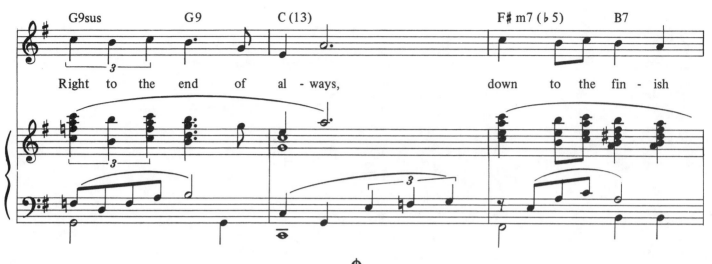

Right to the end of al-ways, down to the fin-ish

line. We Can Make It

We Can Make It

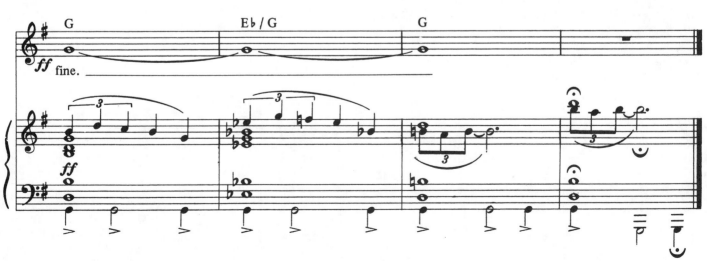

MARRY ME

Words by
FRED EBB

Music by
JOHN KANDER

neigh - bor - hood _____ would give its con - sent,

and there's a cut - a - way _____ I'm dy - ing to

rent
(sung) So Mar - ry Me. _____ Give in and

the day you Mar - ry Me. _____ Give in and

Mar - ry Me.
Mar - ry Me.

I real - ly love you, see? _____ We can't go
Though you don't love me now, _____ you will in

THE RINK

Words by
FRED EBB

Music by
JOHN KANDER

I planned on tak-ing Pol-ly to the pic-ture show.__ But

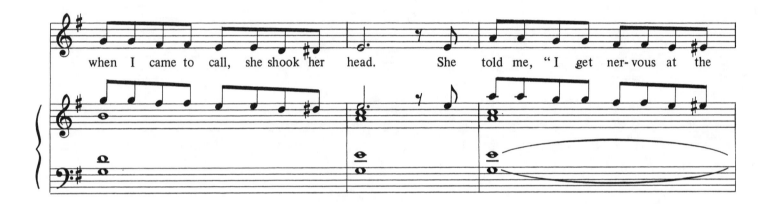

when I came to call, she shook her head. She told me, "I get ner-vous at the

pic - ture show,__ here is where I'd rath - er go in - stead. I

44

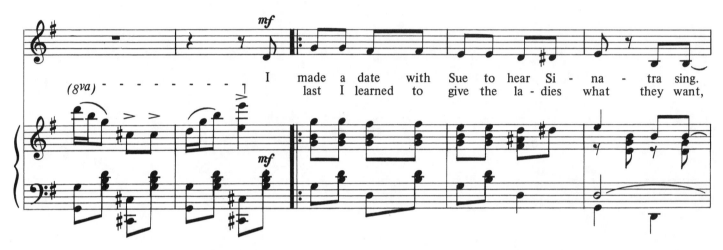

I made a date with Sue to hear Si - na - tra sing.
last I learned to give the la - dies what they want,

She sneered and told me "Frank Si - na - tra?!" Yuk!
and fur - ther - more not throw my dough a - way.

It's just a waste of cash to hear Si - na - tra sing. ___
I'd nev - er take them to a fan - cy rest - au - rant. ___

poco rit.

but   tell me, have you   got a half - a - buck?   Be -

I'd   call them up and   this is what I'd say: "My

Accel. poco a poco

cause,   I   wan - na go 'round The   Rink, The Rink! There's noth - ing to beat The

dear, we're   gon - na go 'round The   Rink, The Rink! There's noth - ing to beat The

Rink, I think. If   I'm gon - na go a - round with you, I   wan - na go 'round The

Rink, I think. If   I'm gon - na go a - round with you, I   wan - na go 'round The

A tempo

Rink!   I   wan - na go see the   spot go pink, I   wan - na go hear the

Rink!   I   wan - na go see the   spot go pink, I   wan - na go hear the

skate key clink. If you wan-na good go 'round with me, we're gon-na go 'round The
skate key clink. If

Rink!

At you wan-na good go

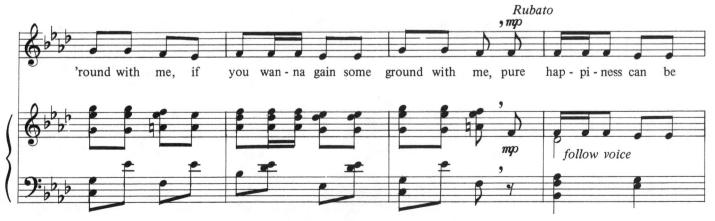

'round with me, if you wan-na gain some ground with me, pure hap-pi-ness can be

found with me by go-ing a - round and 'round and 'round and 'round and 'round and

'round and 'round and 'round and 'round and 'round and 'round and 'round and 'round and

'round and 'round The Rink!"

WALLFLOWER

Words by
FRED EBB

Music by
JOHN KANDER

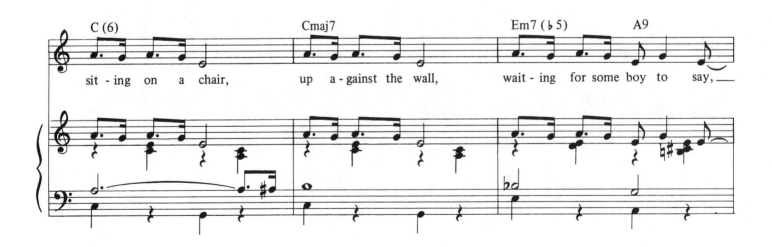

by the crowd. ___ Move, Ba - by, make your bid, ___ and
by the crowd. ___ Shake, Ba - by, make 'em buzz, ___ and

you can heat it up the way your Mom - ma did. ___ Who wants a Wall - flow - er
you can be a whiz the way your Mom - ma was, ___ and not a Wall - flow - er,

wilt - ing in the night hands a - cross your lap, not hav - ing an - y fun at all? ___
wilt - ing in the night, hands a - cross your lap, not hav - ing an - y fun at all! ___

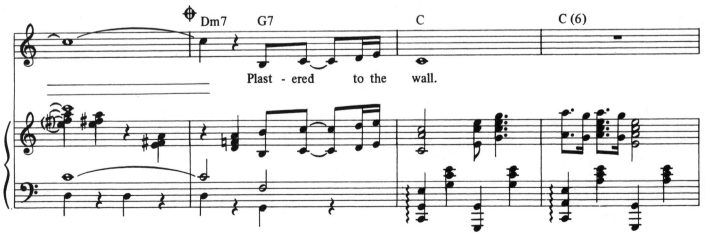

Plast - ered to the wall.

ALL THE CHILDREN IN A ROW

Words by
FRED EBB

Music by
JOHN KANDER

We've a war to win, you know. We've a world to find.

Have you been to Mon-ter-ey? Did-n't Jan-is sing?

rit.

Kes-ey's bus came by to-day. Step-pen-wolf is king.

a tempo

All The Child-ren In A Row, flow-ers in their hair.

Why do peo - ple turn a - way? Man, it is - n't fair.

Lear - y's in the slam - mer now. Boy, is that a

mess. Light a match and burn the card;

Doc - tor Spock says - "Yes!"

Proud - ly march - ing arm in arm sing - ing Dyl - an's songs. No one is a strang - er here,

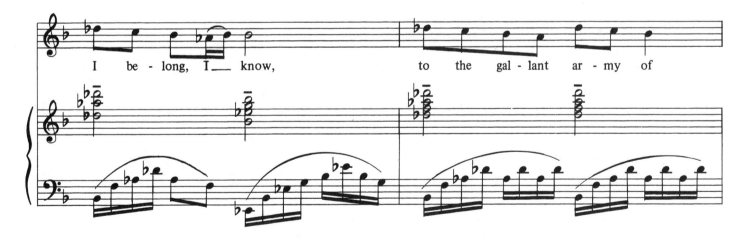

Slower

ev' - ry-one be - longs. Cal - i - forn - ia's warm as love,

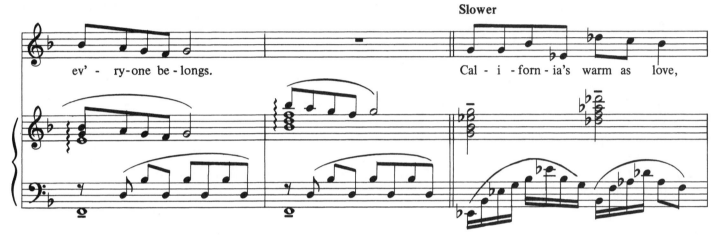

I be - long, I__ know, to the gal - lant ar - my of

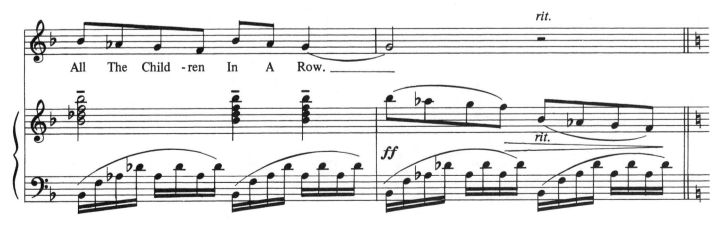

rit.

All The Child - ren In A Row. _____

ff   *rit.*

Who can change things? We can! Who will change things?

We will! And me and Dan -ny run -ning hand in

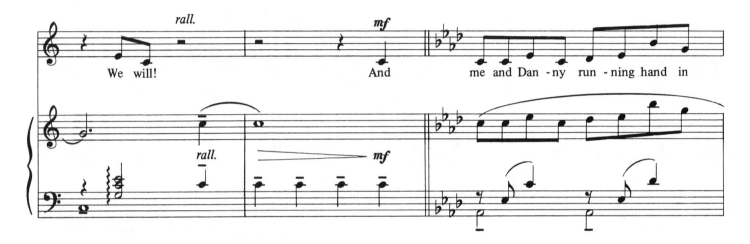

hand, fris- bees on the sand. *(spoken)* *Wanna be my old lady? Whaddya say?*

Me and Dan -ny, bur-gers on a bun, ban -ners in the sun. *(spoken)* *Might as well be my old lady,*
everyone says you are anyway.

(sung) Turn - ing in the night, hun - gry. "Lis - ten, you're my wife, ain't you?

Pro - mise not to laugh, will you? An - swer me one thing, hon - est,

Freely

please don't tell a soul___ I asked___ you. Where's___ Cam - bo- di - a?"___

pp *follow voice*

a tempo
mp

Me and Dan-ny walk -ing down the street. "How we gon - na

rubato
p

a tempo
mp

eat?" (spoken) Dudes who ain't got no old ladies — they move on, ya know? (sung) Me and Dan - ny - "Why'd you pick that

fight? No, it's not all right! We were brave to - geth - er,

strong to - geth - er. Where's it gone?"

Do you need to take that stuff?

Come on, Dan-ny, that's e - nough!

We can make it, we'll sur - vive.   Dan - ny, you're too stoned to

drive!

60

Me and Dan -ny, I don't un -der - stand, where's the world we've

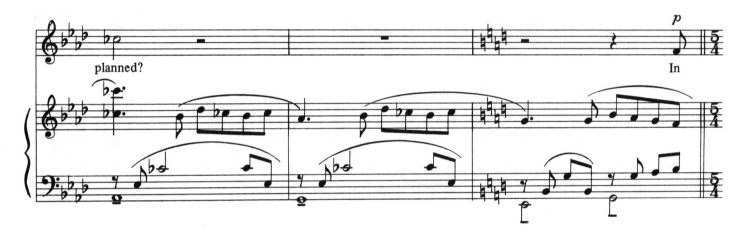

planned? In

Cal - i - forn - ia it does -n't ev -er snow. In Cal - i -forn - ia liv -ing's kind of

slow.

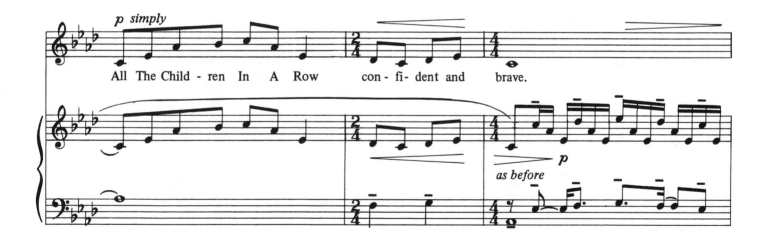

All The Child - ren In A Row con - fi - dent and brave.

We've a war to win, you know. We've a world to

save.　　　　　　　　　　　　　　　　No one thinks we mat - ter much.

No one un - der - stands.　　But we made a dif - f'rence　by the　join - ing of our hands.

Cal - i - forn - ia's　warm as　love.

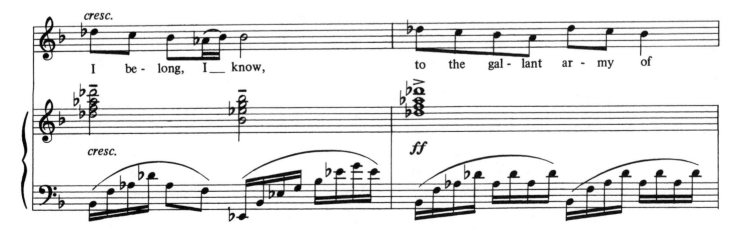

I be - long, I __ know,　　　　　　to the gal - lant ar - my　of

All The Child - ren In A Row.

Freely

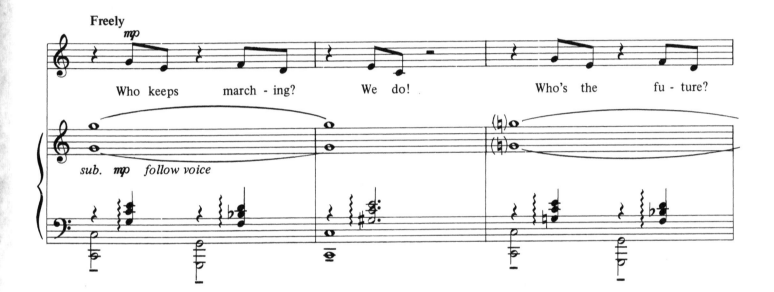

Who keeps march - ing? We do! Who's the fu - ture?

sub. *mp* *follow voice*

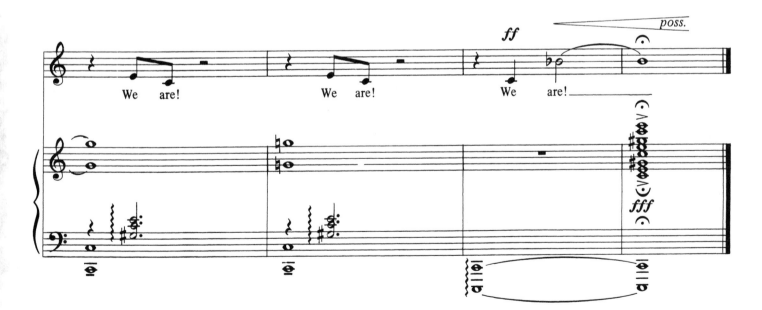

We are! We are! We are!